AF327814

The Bipolar Disorder Journal

The
Bipolar Disorder Journal

Creative Activities to Keep Yourself Well

CARA LISETTE

Foreword by Dr Thomas Richardson
Illustrated by Victoria Barron

Jessica Kingsley Publishers
London and Philadelphia

First published in Great Britain in 2023 by Jessica Kingsley Publishers
An imprint of John Murray Press

1

Copyright © Cara Lisette 2023

The right of Cara Lisette to be identified as the Author of the Work has been asserted
by her in accordance with the Copyright, Designs and Patents Act 1988.

Foreword copyright © Dr Thomas Richardson 2023

Front cover image source: Shutterstock®.

All rights reserved. No part of this publication may be reproduced, stored in a retrieval system,
or transmitted, in any form or by any means without the prior written permission of the
publisher, nor be otherwise circulated in any form of binding or cover other than that in which
it is published and without a similar condition being imposed on the subsequent purchaser.

Disclaimer: The information contained in this book is not intended to replace the
services of trained medical professionals or to be a substitute for medical advice.
You are advised to consult a doctor on any matters relating to your health, and in
particular on any matters that may require diagnosis or medical attention.

A CIP catalogue record for this title is available from the British Library and the Library of Congress

ISBN 978 1 83997 781 7
eISBN 978 1 83997 782 4

Printed and bound in Great Britain by Bell & Bain Limited

Jessica Kingsley Publishers' policy is to use papers that are natural, renewable and recyclable
products and made from wood grown in sustainable forests. The logging and manufacturing
processes are expected to conform to the environmental regulations of the country of origin.

Jessica Kingsley Publishers
Carmelite House
50 Victoria Embankment
London EC4Y 0DZ

www.jkp.com

John Murray Press
Part of Hodder & Stoughton Limited
An Hachette UK Company

Foreword

Bipolar disorder is a mental health problem characterized by episodes of depression where people feel low in mood with no confidence or energy, and episodes of hypomania or mania where there are big ideas, racing thoughts and lots of energy with less need for sleep. It affects at least 2 per cent of people. If you're reading this then I don't need to tell you about the impact it can have on your life in terms of work, relationships, health and finances.

The good news is that we know that psychological therapies such as cognitive behavioural therapy (CBT) are effective for bipolar disorder. They can reduce the risk of relapse and needing to go to hospital. They can help people with everyday functioning, improve your quality of life and help lift you out of depression. Unfortunately, not everyone gets the access to these therapies that they should. Access can depend on where you live, and sometimes whether you can afford it.

It is often the case that health professionals view bipolar disorder as purely biological or genetic illness, and overlook the strong psychological aspects: high standards, self-critical tendencies, goal-focused behaviour when manic. As a result, those with bipolar disorder are often not referred for therapy. They can go in and out of hospital without a lot of support when they are well. They can often end up internalizing this medicalized view that living well with bipolar disorder is only about taking medication. I can't tell you how many people I've worked with who have lived for years, sometimes even decades, with no awareness at all of their triggers and early warning signs of relapse, and no coping strategies other than taking medication. Of course, medication is vital, but there is a lot more that you can do to stay well.

Cara's excellent journal is a really important step in helping those with bipolar disorder feel better able to manage their own condition. It covers important elements such as challenging unhelpful thoughts, identifying early warning signs, coping strategies, the role of inactivity in depression, the importance of involving others in your care and crisis planning. As someone with bipolar disorder myself, and as a clinician working with those with bipolar disorder, I know how important and effective the insights from this book are. These are presented in an accessible and creative way. Developing your own coping strategies, in your own words, displayed in your own way. Use this to personalize your self-care to yourself, making it easier to remember and more directly relevant for you. Completed by you, for you. Living with bipolar disorder can be complicated and confusing; this book and this skills within it are organized, simple and practical.

I hope that this offers a hope to those living with bipolar disorder, as well as being useful for those supporting them, be that loved ones or health professionals. Use this when you are unwell to help yourself feel more in control and help return to stability. Use this when you are stable to help keep it that way. Use it when you are bored or unmotivated to do something creative. Use it when your mind is busy and your mood high to centre and ground. Use it when you are anxious to offload your worries and self-soothe. Don't just complete it once; keep using it, keep coming back to it and updating it when you find new ways to keep yourself well.

I want to thank Cara for inviting me to write this foreword, and I wish all of those reading this foreword all the best for recovery and living well with bipolar disorder.

Dr Thomas Richardson
Associate Professor of Clinical Psychology, University of Southampton, UK

Hello, reader!

Welcome to this journal, which I hope will be a useful tool in managing what can often be a challenging illness to live with. Throughout this book there are a number of exercises to help you to explore different coping strategies, and hopefully to learn more about yourself and your personal experiences of bipolar disorder.

I was diagnosed with bipolar disorder when I was 25, after many years of struggling with my mood and behaving in ways that I didn't always understand. For most of my life I have journaled, and through this process I have learnt a lot about myself and how to manage my illness. The exercises I have included are based on my own experiences, both as a therapist and somebody with bipolar disorder. Over time, these have helped me to spot early warning signs, communicate with others how I am feeling, and improve how I manage both during and after an episode.

This is your book to use as you choose: you can write in it, draw in it, decorate it – creativity is an excellent outlet, and my aim is that you find that some of these prompts bring you closer to where you want to be.

I hope that you are able to get what you want out of this process and that it helps you in your ongoing journey of living the life you want to live.

Never forget that you are more than your illness and that you deserve to live a full and happy life.

Lots of love, Cara

My goals for the future

Start by setting yourself some goals. What would you like to achieve, and by when?

1. ....

....

2. ....

....

3. ....

....

4. ....

....

5. ....

....

6. ....

....

7. ....

....

8. ....

....

9. ....

....

10. ....

....

My reasons to keep going

1. ....

....

2. ....

....

3. ....

....

4. ....

....

5. ....

....

6. ....

....

7. ....

....

8. ....

....

9. ....

....

10. ....

....

YOU
DESERVE
TO BE
HAPPY

Helpful mantras

These feelings are temporary

Tomorrow is a new day

Everything is going to be okay

I am loved

Self-care isn't selfish

My illness does not define me

I deserve to be happy

I can do hard things

Thoughts are not facts

It's okay to say no

Useful distractions

Distractions can be a really useful tool in managing short-term difficult thoughts and feelings. There are some suggestions here that might help, but you will probably have some of your own too.

- Writing
- Drawing
- Reading a book
- Watching a film
- Listening to podcasts or a happy playlist
- Arts and crafts
- Painting your nails
- Having a bath or shower
- Crossword puzzles
- Playing a game
- Colouring books

Distractions that help me

You might already have your own ideas for distraction techniques that help you. Write down some ideas that you could try if you need to take your mind off things.

1. ....
....

2. ....
....

3. ....
....

4. ....
....

5. ....
....

6. ....
....

7. ....
....

8. ....
....

9. ....
....

10. ....
....

You are more than
your illness

How are you feeling today? Draw or write it out!

My mood scale

It can be helpful, when thinking about how to monitor and measure our mood, to think of this on a scale of 0–10. 0 would be the lowest your mood could be and 10 would be the highest your mood could be. What do each of these numbers look like for you? How would you know you were feeling a particular number on the scale, and what might other people notice?

0. ....

....

....

....

1. ....

....

....

....

2. ....

....

....

....

3. ....

....

....

....

4. ....

....

5.

6.

7.

8.

9.

10.

My support network

It's important to reach out for help when we are struggling, whether that be friends, family, mental health professionals or charities, for example. Have a think about who is in your network and who you can reach out to when you need support.

Friends:

....

....

....

....

....

....

....

Family:

....

....

....

....

....

....

....

Professionals:

. . . .

. . . .

. . . .

. . . .

. . . .

. . . .

. . . .

. . . .

Other:

. . . .

. . . .

. . . .

. . . .

. . . .

. . . .

. . . .

YOU MATTER

What is important to me?

When we are struggling with our mental health it can be really difficult to remember what is important to us. Try to make a list of things that are important to you.

1. ....

   ....

2. ....

   ....

3. ....

   ....

4. ....

   ....

5. ....

   ....

6. ....

   ....

7. ....

   ....

8. ....

   ....

9. ....

   ....

10. ....

   ....

What are my values?

Our values are what guide the way we behave, both towards others and towards ourselves. It can be useful to identify our values as this can help us to establish changes we want to make, so we can align our actions closer to the things that are important to us. Here is a list of values that you might connect with. It might help to highlight some, but there is also space to record your own that don't feature here.

Acceptance	Hope	Productivity
Achievement	Independence	Quality
Adventure	Individuality	Quiet
Beauty	Intelligence	Recreation
Bravery	Joy	Reflection
Caring	Justice	Security
Community	Kindness	Spirituality
Compassion	Kinship	Success
Connection	Knowledge	Teamwork
Dedication	Learning	Tolerance
Discovery	Love	Truthfulness
Empowerment	Maturity	Unity
Equality	Morality	Uniqueness
Family	Motivation	Victory
Freedom	Nourishment	Vitality
Fun	Nurture	Wealth
Generosity	Optimism	Wisdom
Growth	Order	Youthfulness
Health	Peace	....
....	....	....
....	....	....
....	....	....
....	....	....

What changes can I make that will bring me
closer to living a life aligned with my values?

Brain dump

How are you feeling right now? Sometimes getting our thoughts out onto the page can help us to process and make sense of them.

Signs I am feeling depressed

How do you know when you are feeling low in mood? What do you, and those around you, need to look out for?

What can I do to help myself when I am feeling depressed?

How can other people help me when I am feeling depressed?

What does depression look like to you?

Try drawing it below.

Setbacks don't
equal failure

Depression hot cross buns

Our thoughts, feelings and behaviours all connect to one another. The way we behave can affect how we think and feel, and trying to change our thinking can impact what we do and what emotions we are experiencing. A 'hot cross bun' is a cognitive behavioural therapy-based exercise that helps us to understand ways we can and do respond in different situations, and what we could do differently next time. There is space to write down your thoughts, emotions, behaviours and physical feelings in each of the boxes. What is a situation you experience when you're feeling depressed? Are there any areas you think you can change to try and improve how you feel?

Current depression situation:

....

....

....

Thoughts

Emotions

Behaviours

Physical sensations

Challenging our thoughts and trying to alter the way we behave in response to difficult emotions can result in improvements to how we feel. What are some alternative thoughts and behaviours you could do in the situation you've chosen, and how might that impact your mood?

What could I do differently in this situation?

. . . .

. . . .

. . . .

Thoughts

Emotions

Behaviours

Physical sensations

YOU GOT THIS!

How are you feeling today? Draw or write it out!

The low mood paradox

When our mood is low, we can often feel unmotivated, lethargic and withdrawn. This can lead to a reduction in our level of activity. For example, we might isolate ourselves socially, stop engaging in hobbies we once enjoyed and even stop attending to important tasks like eating and drinking enough, going to work or education, or paying our bills. However, this then results in us getting stuck in a cycle. What we know is that the more we withdraw from activities, the worse our mood gets. It's completely natural to think that we will start doing these things again once our mood is better, but what we actually need to do is to start engaging in different activities in order to improve our mood.

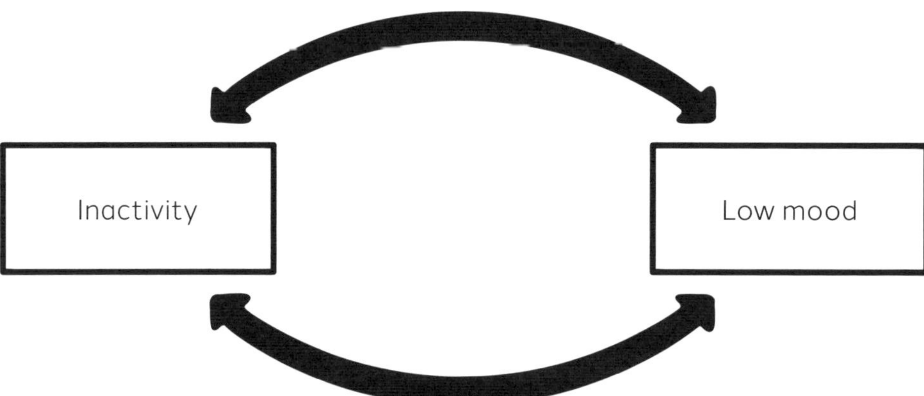

Rather than wait for our mood to improve, we actually need to start doing these actions first. This can feel totally unnatural and go against everything that our minds and bodies feel like they want to do, but it's a really effective way of improving our mood and helping us to regain some energy.

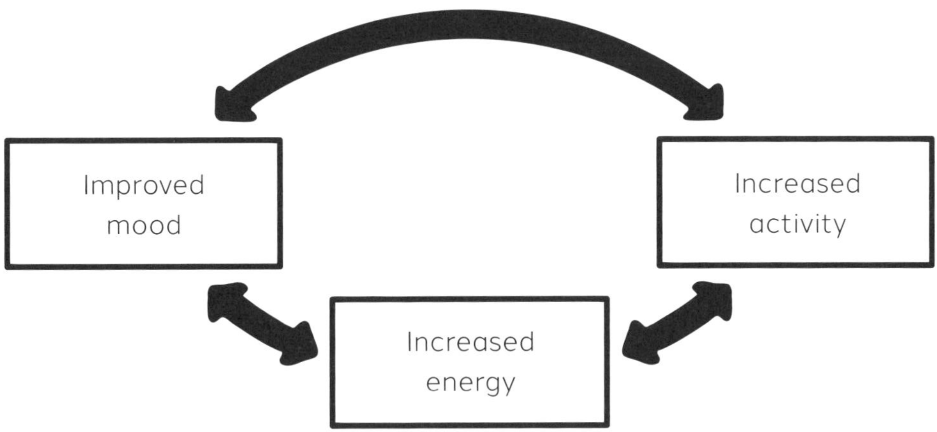

We can break activities down into different categories, for example those which we enjoy including hobbies and relationships, vs those that are more essential life activities such as taking medication or eating regularly. You can sort your activities into whichever categories work for you, but the lists on the following pages might be a helpful guide. Once you have worked out what falls under each category, you can start planning them into your day. It is best to include activities that give you a sense of enjoyment and achievement, as well as those that feel essential but might perhaps be less fun. There will also be some that you find you can manage when you are feeling tired and flat, and others that require a bit more energy.

Activities I enjoy

1.

2.

3.

4.

5.

6.

7.

8.

9.

10.

Activities I need to do

1. ....
   ....

2. ....
   ....

3. ....
   ....

4. ....
   ....

5. ....
   ....

6. ....
   ....

7. ....
   ....

8. ....
   ....

9. ....
   ....

10. ....
    ....

Low-energy activities

1. ....
....

2. ....
....

3. ....
....

4. ....
....

5. ....
....

6. ....
....

7. ....
....

8. ....
....

9. ....
....

10. ....
....

High-energy activities

1.

2.

3.

4.

5.

6.

7.

8.

9.

10.

Scheduling my week

There are lots of different ways to schedule your time. Some people find it easier to do it a day at a time, others a week at a time, and you might prefer to do it hour by hour or break it down in to bigger chunks. Here is a guide to get you started.

	Monday	Tuesday	Wednesday
Morning activities			
Afternoon activities			
Evening activities			

Thursday	Friday	Saturday	Sunday

Letter writing

When we feel low, it's really common to start feeling negatively towards ourselves and about life in general. What would you like to say to yourself when you next feel this way?

THERE IS GOOD IN THE WORLD
BECAUSE YOU ARE
HERE

Signs I am feeling hypomanic or manic

How do you know when you are feeling high in mood? What do you, and those around you, need to look out for?

What can I do to help myself when I am feeling manic?

How can other people help me when I am feeling manic?

Activities that make me feel calm

1. ....

....

2. ....

....

3. ....

....

4. ....

....

5. ....

....

6. ....

....

7. ....

....

8. ....

....

9. ....

....

10. ....

....

Keep going

What does mania look like to you?

Try drawing it below.

Mania hot cross buns

As previously discussed, our thoughts, feelings and behaviours all connect to one another. The way we behave can affect how we think and
feel, and trying to change our thinking can impact what we do and what
emotions we are experiencing. What is a situation you experience when
you're feeling manic? Are there any areas you think you can change to
try and improve how you feel?

Current mania situation:

....

....

....

....

Thoughts

Emotions

Behaviours

Physical
sensations

What are some alternative thoughts and behaviours you could do in the situation you've chosen, and how might that impact your mood?

What could you do differently in this situation?

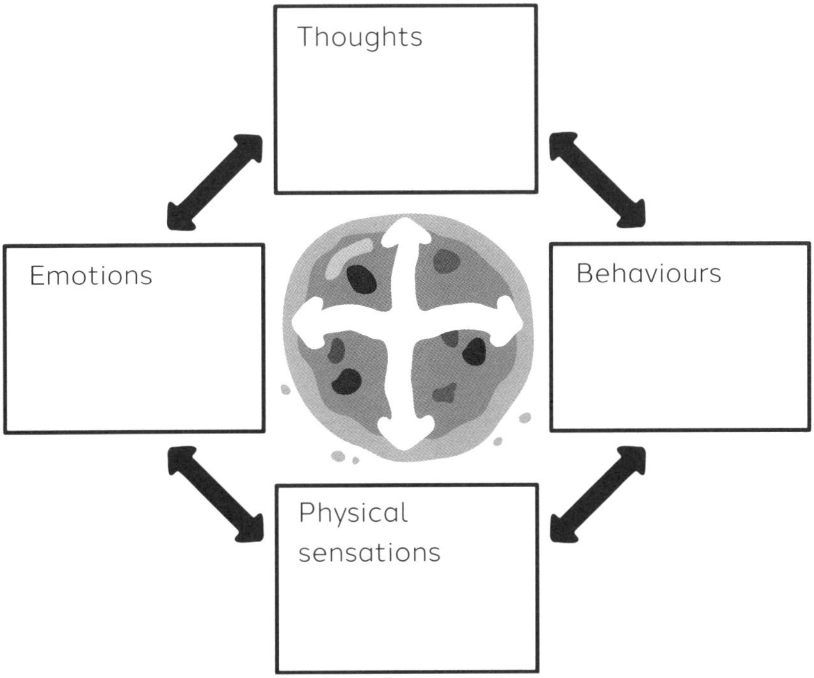

....

....

....

Thoughts

Emotions

Behaviours

Physical sensations

Coping with psychosis

While not everybody with bipolar disorder will experience episodes of psychosis, it is something that affects a lot of people, both when manic and when depressed. It can be useful to have a think about what could be helpful for you if this does occur, and what it is that you need to help you to get through it.

How would I know if I were becoming psychotic?

....

....

....

....

....

....

What would I like to say to future me who is experiencing psychosis?

....

....

....

....

....

What do I need to do when I am experiencing psychosis?

What do I need from others when I am experiencing psychosis?

HEALING
ISN'T
LINEAR

Letter writing

When our mood is elevated, it can be hard to remember the downfalls and difficulties that come with mania. What would you like to say to yourself when you next feel this way?

Brain dump

How are you feeling right now? Sometimes getting our thoughts out onto the page can help us to process and make sense of them.

Pros and cons

Often, when people are experiencing elevated mood, it can feel like it's really important to start new projects, spend lots of money and make big, impulsive decisions. It can be helpful to work out what the costs vs the benefits are of these decisions, to see if we really want to go through with them. It can be especially useful to go through this exercise with somebody else, to gain a different perspective.

Writing it down can be really useful when working out the details of decision making.

What are the pros of this decision?	What are the cons of this decision?
What am I trying to achieve?	What resources do I need?
What steps do I need to take?	What would I say to a friend who wanted to do this?

Mood diary

Keeping a mood diary can be a really useful tool when we are trying to prevent episodes occurring by noticing any early warning signs. You can keep this diary in whatever way feels helpful, but the template below might give you a starting point. It includes different things I like to keep track of when monitoring my wellbeing.

	Monday	Tuesday	Wednesday
Mood (0–10)			
Anxiety (0–10)			
Hours slept			
Medication taken (Y/N)			
Significant event (Y/N)			
Eaten enough (Y/N)			
Hydrated enough (Y/N)			
Alcohol (Y/N)			
Other substances (Y/N)			
Other relevant information			

Thursday	Friday	Saturday	Sunday

What does a stable mood look like for me?

What would you, or other people, say about how you feel and behave when your mood is stable?

Things I like about myself

Low self-esteem is often something that occurs alongside mental health difficulties. Try to think of some qualities you like about yourself that you can reflect on in future.

1. ....
....

2. ....
....

3. ....
....

4. ....
....

5. ....
....

6. ....
....

7. ....
....

8. ....
....

9. ....
....

10. ....
....

Things other people like about me

It can also be helpful to reflect on things other people value in us, as they may be different to our own. Ask the people around you what they like about you – some of the answers might surprise you.

1. ....
....

2. ....
....

3. ....
....

4. ....
....

5. ....
....

6. ....
....

7. ....
....

8. ....
....

9. ....
....

10. ....
....

Self-care activities

It can feel difficult to look after ourselves when we are struggling with our mental health. One of the best ways to challenge this is to start being kind to ourselves. What self-care activities can you try?

1. ....

....

2. ....

....

3. ....

....

4. ....

....

5. ....

....

6. ....

....

7. ....

....

8. ....

....

9. ....

....

10. ....

....

31 days of self-care

1 Think about an area where you need to set boundaries	**2** Write down three things you like about your personality	**3** Forgive yourself
8 Take five minutes to have a cup of tea	**9** Think of something nice you have done for someone recently	**10** Have a social media detox day
15 Eat something nourishing	**16** Do ten minutes of exercise	**17** List three of your role models and the qualities you admire about them
22 Watch something that will make you laugh	**23** Think about the last positive thing somebody said about you	**24** Go outside and look at the night sky
29 Reach out to a friend	**30** Think of three positive words other people would use to describe you	**31** What would you say to your inner child?

4 Say yes to something	**5** Start your day with a positive affirmation	**6** List three things that make you happy to be alive	**7** Spend time outside
11 Think about what your younger self would be proud of you for	**12** Write down something you have done well today	**13** Get up early to watch the sunrise	**14** Do five minutes of relaxation or mindfulness
18 Have an early night	**19** Make a list of all of your achievements today	**20** Declutter and tidy your safe space	**21** Think about one way you make the world a better place
25 Think about the last time you did something nice for somebody	**26** Cook something nice for yourself	**27** Take half an hour to read a book	**28** Find three motivational quotes that mean something to you

Quotes, lyrics and phrases that inspire me

How are you feeling today? Draw or write it out!

Why do I want to stay well?

What are your reasons for wanting to focus on keeping yourself well?

Current coping strategies

It's likely that over time you will have picked up some coping strategies for when things get difficult. However, it's important to remember that these might not always be healthy or beneficial to us in the long term, even though they might help us in the short term. Hopefully, you will also have some that are helpful for you in both the immediate and the future. Have a think through the coping strategies you currently use, and whether these are helpful for both present and future you.

Coping strategy:

....

....

Short-term pros:

....

....

Short-term cons:

....

....

Long-term pros:

....

....

Long-term cons:

....

....

Coping strategy:

....

....

Short-term pros:

....

....

Short-term cons:

....

....

Long-term pros:

....

....

Long-term cons:

....

....

Coping strategy:

....

....

Short-term pros:

....

....

Short-term cons:

....

....

Long-term pros:

....

....

Long-term cons:

....

....

New coping strategies

Are there any coping strategies that you haven't tried yet, that you think might be helpful? List them below, and revisit this page next time you feel you need it.

1. ....
....

2. ....
....

3. ....
....

4. ....
....

5. ....
....

6. ....
....

7. ....
....

8. ....
....

9. ....
....

10. ....
....

THOUGHTS
ARE
NOT
FACTS

54321 grounding technique

Anxiety and distress can feel completely overwhelming sometimes. If you find yourself feeling like this, this technique can be very effective at bringing you back into the here and now by helping you to connect to your senses. There are five steps to follow.

1. Look around you and notice **five things you can see**. This could be a painting, a plant or a person, for example. Pay attention to what each of these things look like: their shapes, colours and sizes.

2. Focus on **four things you can feel**. This could be the wind, your clothes against your skin, the floor underneath your feet. Notice the different textures and sensations.

3. Name **three things you can hear**. Maybe there are birds chirping outside, or cars passing in the street. Perhaps you can hear a TV show in the background. Focus on the different tones and volumes.

4. Notice **two things you can smell**. Have you used a nice fabric softener on your clothes, or are you wearing your favourite perfume? Maybe you are outdoors and can smell plants and flowers.

5. Think about **one thing you can taste**. Perhaps you have chewing gum or a cup of tea nearby. If you can't taste anything, try to imagine what one of your favourite things tastes like.

The power of music

Music can be an amazing tool for our wellbeing, and there are so many inspiring songs and artists out there. The type of music we listen to can have a big impact on our mood, and it would be helpful to think about what songs might help you when you need a bit of motivation, as well as when you feel you need some calm.

My motivational playlist:

....

....

....

....

....

....

....

My relaxing playlist:

....

....

....

....

....

....

My skills and strengths

Everybody has their own individual strengths that we can draw upon when things feel difficult. What are some of yours? If you feel stuck, it can help to ask the people around you their thoughts.

1. ....
....

2. ....
....

3. ....
....

4. ....
....

5. ....
....

6. ....
....

7. ....
....

8. ....
....

9. ....
....

10. ....
....

Brain dump

How are you feeling right now? Sometimes getting our thoughts out onto the page can help us to process and make sense of them.

Sleep hygiene

Sleep hygiene is just a term that means 'good sleeping habits'. I'm sure you know how important regular sleep is for keeping your mood stable, but it can be a difficult thing to achieve in practice when we have busy lives.

The most helpful thing to do is to get yourself into a consistent bedtime routine. This should occur at the same time every night, if possible. Prior to going to bed, you should try to avoid large meals, caffeine and blue light from electronics such as phones or tablets.

It can also help to do calming activities such as having a bath, reading and turning down very bright lights.

Getting exercise during the day can also help with falling asleep, in addition to a dark, quiet room which is at a comfortable temperature.

It's important to try to wake up at the same time every morning too, and to avoid taking naps during the day, as this gets us into a regular sleep cycle.

Are there any changes you think you need to make to your bedtime routine? Think about how you could improve your sleep below.

What could your helpful bedtime routine look like?

Be gentle with
yourself – you're doing
the best you can

Unhelpful thinking traps

Most of us have thinking habits that we have developed over our lives, and these can sometimes get in the way when we are feeling distressing and difficult emotions. These are some of the most common ones that people experience.

Mind reading:

Assuming we know what other people are thinking.

Example: 'They all think I am stupid.'

Ask yourself: Am I making assumptions about what they are thinking?

Prediction:

Thinking we know what's going to happen in the future.

Example: 'I am going to fail that assignment.'

Ask yourself: How likely is it that this is going to happen?

Comparing and despairing:

Only seeing the positives in others then comparing ourselves against them negatively.

Example: 'I am rubbish at drawing compared to them.'

Ask yourself: Am I focusing on others rather than myself?

<h2 align="center">Mental filter:</h2>

Only noticing what we want to notice and filtering out everything else that doesn't fit that narrative, like sieving out all the positives and only letting the negatives through.

Example: Only noticing things we consider to be our failures and ignoring any successes.

Ask yourself: Am I only noticing the bad things?

<h2 align="center">Mountains and molehills:</h2>

Exaggerating the negatives and minimizing the positives.

Example: Thinking the negatives are worse than they are and the positives are less significant than they are.

Ask yourself: What would somebody else say about this situation?

<h2 align="center">Critical self:</h2>

Putting ourselves down and blaming ourselves for things that are not our fault – also referred to as the 'internal bully'.

Example: 'The group project not going well at work is all my fault.'

Ask yourself: What role did others play in this situation?

<h2 align="center">Shoulds and musts:</h2>

Putting pressure on ourselves and having unreasonable or unrealistic expectations of what we should or shouldn't be doing.

Example: 'I should be good at this by now.'

Ask yourself: Is this an unrealistic expectation I am setting for myself?

Black and white thinking:

Thinking that things can only be right or wrong, good or bad, with nothing in between.

Example: 'If I don't do this perfectly then I have failed.'

Ask yourself: Is it possible to do everything perfectly all of the time?

Catastrophizing:

Believing or imagining only the worst possible case scenario.

Example: 'This is going to be a disaster.'

Ask yourself: What are some other possible outcomes to this situation?

Labelling:

Giving labels to others or to ourselves.

Example: 'I am an idiot.'

Ask yourself: What would somebody else say in this situation?

Emotional reasoning:

Assuming our feelings are always rational; for example, 'I am anxious so I must be in danger.'

Example: 'I feel ashamed so I must be a bad person.'

Ask yourself: Does feeling bad mean something is bad?

Overgeneralizing:

Noticing a pattern based on one situation or drawing wide-ranging conclusions.

Example: 'Nothing good ever happens.'

Ask yourself: What positive things have happened?

Personalization:

Taking responsibility or feeling a sense of blame for something that may not be your fault.

Example: 'It's my fault that my friendship group fell out.'

Ask yourself: Were there any other factors involved in this situation happening?

Everybody has their own individual traps – you might find some of these don't apply to you at all and others make complete sense. It might be helpful to think about which of them feel relevant to you and situations where you think they might arise. For example, if you find yourself feeling very anxious about things that could happen in the future, you might be 'catastrophizing' or 'predicting'. The more you start to recognize your own thinking traps, the more you can start to challenge them.

What are my unhelpful thinking styles?

When might I notice them?

How does this affect me?

Square breathing technique

Square breathing has been shown to be helpful when trying to relax and feel calm, and it is an exercise that can be used wherever you are. Find a window, a wall, a painting or any other square shape you can see to focus on. If you can't find one, you can use your index finger to trace one in front of you.

Slowly trace your eyes across the top of the square in front of you, breathing in for a count of four. As you scan down the right side of the square, hold your breath for a count of four. Breathe out for a count of four as you trace the bottom of the square, then hold for a count of four as you scan up the left-hand side. Repeat this as many times as necessary, breathing in a slow and controlled way.

How are you feeling today? Draw or write it out!

Communicating with others

When we are struggling with our mental health, we can often end up isolating ourselves from others. This can make it difficult for people to help us, because they either don't know we are feeling this distress or they aren't sure exactly how to help.

How could you communicate how you are feeling with people when you are finding things difficult?

How to make a self-soothe box

Self-soothe boxes, also referred to as crisis boxes or sensory boxes, are excellent tools to have access to. They are designed to be full of items that help you to get through periods of distress. Try to fill yours with things that cater to each of your five senses. Here are some suggestions of things you could include that might be helpful:

- **Taste:** Chocolates or mints, or maybe your favourite teabags
- **Smell:** Essential oils, nice hand creams or perfume
- **Touch:** Stress balls, tangles or something soft like a small cuddly toy
- **Hear:** A prompt card to remind you to access your happy playlist or favourite song
- **See:** Photos of people you love, motivational quotes or perhaps some letters of encouragement

It might also be helpful to keep a list of distractions, helplines or apps that you find useful when you are finding things difficult.

What will go in my self-soothe box?

TOMORROW IS A NEW DAY

What would I say to a friend if they were going through this?

Having an illness like bipolar disorder, which can affect many areas of our lives and those around us, can often result in feelings of guilt and we can be harder on ourselves than we need to be. It's also easy to be unkind to ourselves when we are feeling depressed or struggling to cope after a mood episode. Remember, it's not your fault that you have a mental illness. What would you say to a friend if they were going through something similar?

It's okay to ask
for help

People who inspire me

We can draw inspiration from lots of different places, but sometimes having people we look up to can be really helpful. Who inspires you to be your best self?

1.

2.

3.

4.

5.

6.

7.

8.

9.

10.

Checking in with myself

It's not uncommon to find it difficult to pin down or connect with how we are feeling, which can make it difficult to spot early warning signs of relapses. The following steps can help you to notice how you might feel at that moment.

What am I feeling in my body right now?

What emotions can I feel right now?

What thoughts are going through my mind in this moment?

....

....

....

....

....

....

....

What am I doing now?

....

....

....

....

....

....

....

What do I want for myself going forward?

....

....

....

....

....

....

Positive words wordsearch

The first three words you see are your words of the day.

F	M	A	I	E	D	W	J	B	R	A	V	E	I
L	A	T	Y	H	B	I	B	K	U	L	N	E	H
O	C	S	K	A	R	N	E	I	X	C	G	J	E
U	C	I	T	O	E	I	C	N	K	W	Z	H	A
R	E	P	K	V	A	A	O	D	B	E	G	Z	L
I	P	Z	X	Z	D	T	S	N	L	Y	F	D	I
S	T	F	O	R	G	I	V	E	N	E	S	S	N
H	A	P	P	I	N	E	S	S	M	N	J	Z	G
I	N	U	H	S	F	R	Y	S	L	N	H	C	M
N	C	Z	P	D	C	H	J	P	R	V	V	L	Z
G	E	D	C	N	M	I	N	D	F	U	L	O	C
H	R	T	T	A	P	E	A	C	E	F	U	L	O
X	Q	P	O	S	I	T	I	V	I	T	Y	P	G
I	Q	D	S	P	F	C	A	L	M	F	V	B	R

HAPPINESS

FLOURISHING

FORGIVENESS

POSITIVITY

PEACEFUL

CALM

MINDFUL

HEALING

ACCEPTANCE

BRAVE

KINDNESS

Letter writing

Living with bipolar disorder can frequently bring up lots of emotions for us, from fear and anger to acceptance and relief. There are often lots of thoughts swimming around, not just soon after diagnosis but throughout our lives. If you could write a letter to your illness, what would you say?

What are my triggers?

We all have triggers that can lead to lapses and relapses, and it's important to remember that different situations and experiences are likely to contribute to different mood episodes. Writing them down can help us to recognize them, so we can then learn to challenge and cope with them when they arise.

What are my triggers for depressive episodes?

What are my triggers for manic episodes?

How can I cope with my triggers?

Once we have identified triggers, we can start to notice them more. The world can be a difficult place at times and sometimes we are going to come across things that trigger us. How can you cope with or manage yours?

Doing your best
is enough

My traffic lights

Sometimes it can be helpful to think of our progress in terms of a traffic light system: red meaning relapse, orange meaning we need to be careful and pay more attention to our thoughts and feelings, and green meaning we are well and happy. Have a think about what life looks like for you in each of these zones and what your plan of action would be for each one.

What does my green zone look like?

....
....
....
....

How can I stay in this zone?

....
....
....
....

What does my orange zone look like?

....
....
....
....

How can I get out of this zone?

What does my red zone look like?

How can I get out of this zone?

Early warning signs

Sometimes – often even – it can feel like a mood episode has come out of nowhere. However, it's likely that there are some early warning signs that a lapse or relapse is approaching, even if we don't always realize it. What do you think you, or those around you, might notice ahead of this happening?

Early warning signs that I am becoming depressed

Early warning signs that I am becoming manic

How are you feeling today? Draw or write it out!

Keeping myself safe

Although this doesn't apply to everybody, there are times when we are unwell that there may be risks to our safety, either from ourselves or from others. If this applies to you, what do you think those risks are, and how can you keep yourself safe?

Crisis planning

It's perfectly possible that our moods will fluctuate without each of those episodes resulting in a crisis; however, it's important to be prepared should that situation arise. Have a think, either alone or with people around you, about how you would manage if you felt you were in crisis.

What signs should I be aware of if I am heading to a crisis?

....

....

....

....

What signs should other people be aware of if I am heading to a crisis?

....

....

....

....

What can I do to manage this without needing direct support from another person?

....

....

....

....

Who can I contact if I am in crisis?

What do I need from those people?

Where can I go if I am in crisis?

How can I keep my environment safe if I am in crisis?

Brain dump

How are you feeling right now? Sometimes getting our thoughts out onto the page can help us to process and make sense of them.

Remember how
far you've come

Keeping well

There are lots of things we need to do to keep ourselves on track, some every day and some less often. Have a think about what some of these are for you.

What can I do on a daily basis to keep myself well?

What can I do on a weekly basis to keep myself well?

What do I need to do less often to keep myself well?

Managing setbacks

Bipolar disorder is an illness with symptoms that will fluctuate across our lifetime, and it's likely we are all going to have things that happen in our lives that require us to use our coping skills, whatever those may be. Have a think about what might lead to a setback for you, and how you would manage it.

What could cause a setback?

How could I manage this?

REACHING
OUT
IS
BRAVE

What have I achieved since starting this journal?

I hope that over the time you have been working through this book, you have been able to start thinking more about ways you can manage your bipolar disorder. What are some of the things you have achieved, no matter how big or small, since you started using this journal?

Congratulations, reader!

You've worked your way through this journal. I hope that you have found some of these exercises useful and that they have got you thinking about ways you can live the life you deserve because of, and in spite of, bipolar disorder.

There are ways you can continue seeking support, which you will find at the back of this book.

I wish you all the luck in the world for your life beyond this journal. Remember, you are more than just your illness. Be kind to yourself.

Lots of love, Cara

Useful Resources

UK

Bipolar UK: www.bipolaruk.org

Mind: www.mind.org.uk / 0300 123 3393

Samaritans: www.samaritans.org / 116 123

USA

International Bipolar Foundation: www.ibpf.org / 1-800-273-8255

Australia

Bipolar Australia: www.bipolaraustralia.org.au / 13 11 14

Acknowledgements

There are lots of people to thank for the role they have played in my journey with bipolar disorder. My adolescence was very difficult and felt very chaotic at times, and I often felt like I was different to other people. I spent a lot of time in deep episodes of depression, but I never felt like that fully answered the question of 'what is wrong with me?'

When I was diagnosed with bipolar disorder at 25, my initial reaction was a mixture of fear and relief at the same time. I finally felt like parts of my life made sense, although I did feel overwhelmed at knowing this was something I would be managing long term. I now don't consider this illness as 'something that is wrong with me', but just one part of many different factors that make me the person I am today.

Despite all the ups and downs that this illness has thrown at me, especially before I was diagnosed and received treatment for it, I have a wonderful support network who have stuck by me no matter how challenging that might have been at times.

So, thanks of course go to the mental health professionals who have supported me since my childhood. But most of all thank you to my partner, my best friends and my family for standing by me no matter what. Thank you for offering to cook and clean for me when I've been too unwell to take care of myself. Thank you for helping me to bounce back when I feel like I'm never going to get back on track, and for reminding me that there is more to me than this illness. I am forever grateful for each and every one of you.

About the Author

Cara Lisette had struggled with her mood from her early teens but wasn't diagnosed with bipolar disorder until her mid-20s. Through finally discovering the answer to why she felt different to other people, and the subsequent support from mental health services that followed, she has been able to learn about how to manage her illness, and how to be kind to herself when she does experience lapses and relapses.

Cara has long been creative and kept journals for many years, and she has found solace and value in creativity as a way to express thoughts and feelings. It is through doing this that she discovered how this could impact her ability to recognize different strategies that she uses to keep well and live the life she wants to live.

She put this book together with the hope that others would discover the role that creativity can play in maintaining positive mental health and that it might help people to learn more about themselves and their illness and, in turn, skills to cope when things do get difficult.

Cara is also a registered mental health nurse and qualified psychological therapist, so throughout this book you will find exercises and tools that she has not only found helpful in her own journey, but knowledge she can draw upon from her experiences of working as a mental health professional.

She runs a successful blog (www.caras-corner.com) about her experiences with mental illness and can be found on Twitter and Instagram at @caralisette, where you can follow her progress in more detail and keep up to date with her other projects.

From the author

The Eating Disorder Recovery Journal

Cara Lisette
Foreword by Dr Emily David
Illustrated by Victoria Barron

The Eating Disorder Recovery Journal is designed to help you to understand your eating disorder better and to support you in your recovery journey. It is packed full of activities, such as writing prompts, colouring pages and crafting ideas, as well as motivational quotes and positive affirmations to help keep you on track. Drawing on evidence-based techniques including CBT and mindfulness, it brings together creative activities and approaches that have helped author Cara Lisette to challenge her eating disorder, stay motivated, improve body image and prevent relapses.

This journal is yours to be as free and creative with as you wish. It is designed for anybody struggling with an eating disorder who wants to start their recovery journey and reclaim their freedom and future.

£14.99 | $19.95 | PB | 128pp | ISBN 978 1 83997 085 6 | eISBN 978 1 83997 086 3

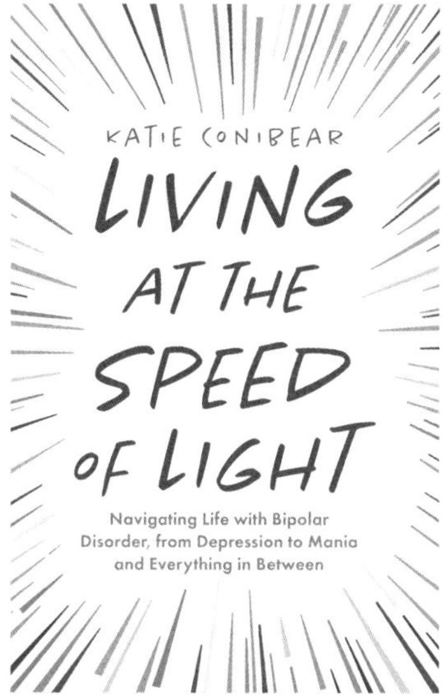

Living at the Speed of Light
Navigating Life with Bipolar Disorder, from Depression to Mania
and Everything in Between

Katie Conibear

Shining a light on mania, depression and everything in between, this no-nonsense guide to life with bipolar disorder gives advice on how to manage the condition and work towards stability.

Drawing on her own experiences, Katie Conibear discusses the realities of life with bipolar and shares practical tips and advice. She explains different symptoms, including mania, hypomania, psychosis and depression, and gives advice on managing relationships, facing stigma and discrimination and learning to be comfortable with stability. The book also contains a chapter on how friends, family and caregivers can support someone with bipolar practically.

Whether you suspect you have bipolar disorder, have been recently diagnosed or have been living with the condition for many years, this honest but hopeful guide is a must read.

£14.99 | $20.95 | PB | 192pp | ISBN 978 1 78775 557 4 | eISBN 978 1 78775 558 1